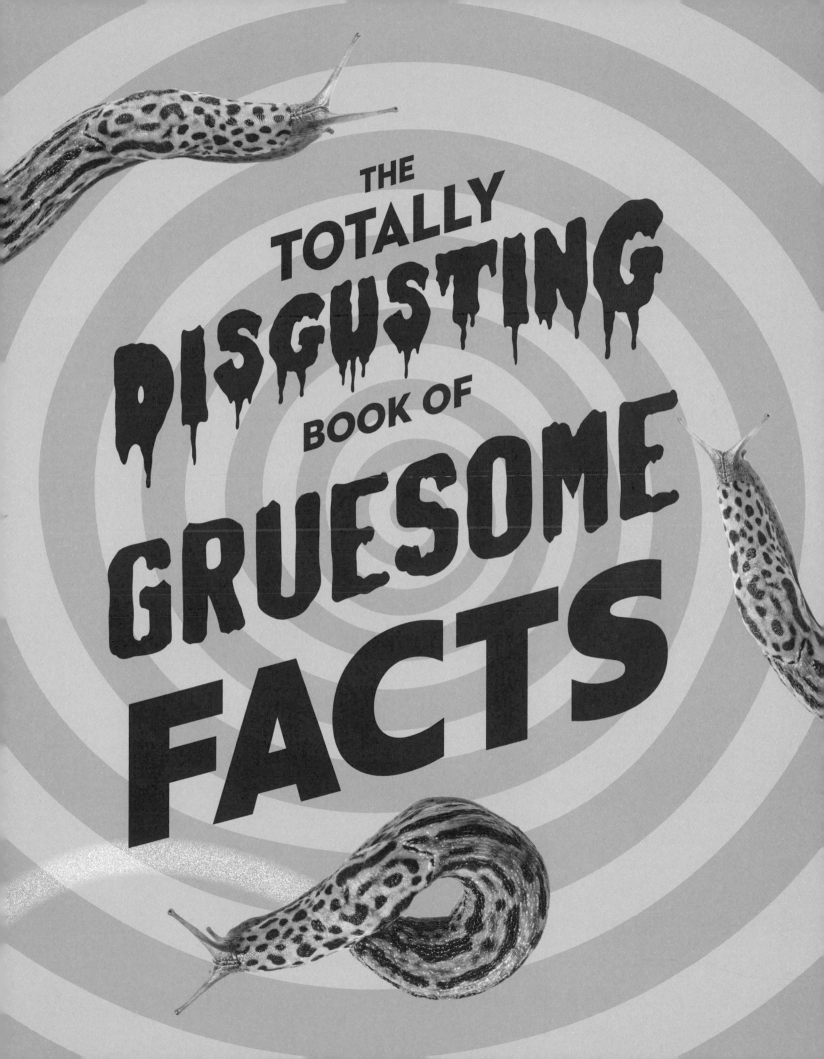

THE TOTALLY DISGUSTING BOOK OF GRUESOME FACTS

AUTUMN
PUBLISHING

Produced by Tall Tree Books
Written by Katie Dicker
Cover designed by Richard Sykes
Designed by Richard Sykes and Jonathon Vipond
Edited by Rebecca Kealy

Copyright © 2023 Igloo Books Ltd

Published in 2023
First published in the UK by Autumn Publishing
An imprint of Igloo Books Ltd
Cottage Farm, NN6 0BJ, UK
Owned by Bonnier Books
Sveavägen 56, Stockholm, Sweden

Manufactured in China. 0823 001
10 9 8 7 6 5 4 3 2 1

Library of Congress Cataloging-in-Publication
Data is available upon request.

ISBN 9781837716838
autumnpublishing.co.uk
bonnierbooks.co.uk

THE TOTALLY DISGUSTING BOOK OF GRUESOME FACTS

AUTUMN PUBLISHING

CONTENTS

HORRENDOUS HISTORY

NAUSEOUS NATURE

FOUL FOOD

BRUTAL BODY BITS

From snot, sweat, and saliva to pus and poop, we're not a pretty sight! Let's get up close and personal with blood and bacteria, mucus and mites, digestive juices and dead skin—just be sure to hold down the vomit!

CLOSE INSPECTION

page 8

page 10

OPEN WIDE

CLOSE INSPECTION

Even when you're sparkling clean, your body is teeming with life!

HAIR-RAISING!

It doesn't matter how clean you are, you'll still have around 1 million mites living on your body hair—even your eyelashes!

These microscopic creatures live naturally at the base of our hairs, feeding on skin oils and dead skin cells.

GOT AN ITCH?
Usually, the mites aren't a problem, but if you get too many, they'll make you itch.

Tiny bacteria are dwarfed by flakes of dead skin.

GROSS FACT ALERT!
There are more than **2,000** different bacteria species living in your belly button alone!

HOTTER HANDS

Doorknobs and handrails may look clean, but they're full of viruses and bacteria.

These microbes can enter our body if we prepare our food with dirty hands, or touch our eyes, nose, or mouth.

There are about 1.5 trillion bacteria living on your skin.

NOW WASH YOUR HANDS! On average, our hands carry over **3,000** different germs from the surfaces we touch.

NAILED IT?

Your fingernails are the perfect breeding ground for bacteria. They give extra protection and a cozy, moist space.

Keeping nails short and clean is the best defense. And as for biting your nails—don't go there!

SKIN CRAWLING

Your skin is home to an army of bacteria. Many of them feast on the sweat under your armpits and on your feet. Who said socks weren't stinky?

These harmless bacteria are our buddies and form the first line of defense against harmful bacteria. So it's good to be teeming with life!

DID YOU KNOW? There are **32** types of bacteria and **28** different fungi living beneath our fingernails.

OPEN WIDE

Say cheese—but don't look too closely!

STINKY BREATH

All day and night, tiny microbes feed on the food between your teeth.

These bacteria can cause stinky breath, which is made worse if you have gum disease or an infection.

As for strong-smelling foods, such as onion and garlic, you're better off keeping a distance!

FREAKY FACT!
There are more bacteria in your mouth than there are humans on Earth!

TONGUE TWISTER

Sometimes, the surface of your tongue can have a yucky yellow crust—a harmless build-up of dead skin cells.

These become trapped in the tiny hair-like projections on the tongue (called papillae), but a quick brush usually does the trick.

Food coloring can cause a stronger shade, as can sugary drinks and some medicines.

These pointy objects are papillae seen close-up.

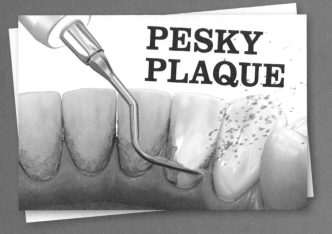

PESKY PLAQUE

We all have a sticky film called plaque on our teeth, which builds up if we don't brush properly.

The bacteria in plaque thrive on our food and produce acid, causing havoc with our teeth and gums. Best get rid of those bad boys with a regular brush!

PROBLEM PLAQUE
Plaque is formed when saliva mixes with leftover food particles, especially sugary or starchy foods.

SWEET TREATS

Next time you reach for a can of soda, think about your pearly whites! Citric acid and other acidic ingredients can attack your tooth enamel and cause cavities, even in sugar-free varieties.

The bacteria in your mouth love to gorge on these drinks, so don't give them a regular feast! And if you do, be sure to brush a little extra.

GRUESOME GUT

Your digestive system works overtime to process what you eat.

STRETCHY STORAGE

Your stomach expands and contracts every time you fill and empty your esophagus.

Did you know it takes **8 hours** for some food to pass from your stomach to your intestines? That's more than a full day at school!

SUPER SIZE
An empty stomach is about the size of your fist, but it can stretch to hold a whopping **1 gallon** of food!

Mouth

Esophagus

Liver

Stomach

Gallbladder

Pancreas

Small intestine

Anus

Large intestine

POO-EY!

Adults produce about a quart of gas a day—enough farts to fill a party balloon in a week!

Your digestive system absorbs the nutrients your body needs, and gets rid of waste.

If you swallow extra air, you'll burp it up, but sometimes it mixes with fermented bacteria and goes the other way. This gas is extra smelly if you've eaten sulfur-rich foods.

WHAT IS BILE?

An adult liver can weigh up to **4 lbs.**

Your liver makes "bile"—a digestive liquid full of enzymes that break down your food into smaller and smaller parts, which your body can absorb. It's the pigment in bile that gives your poop its brown color.

If fats weren't broken down by these clever enzymes, they'd congeal in your guts. Thankfully, your body works its magic and you can absorb them.

WORM TALES

Tapeworms can enter your digestive system if you eat raw or undercooked meat from an animal that's eaten tapeworm eggs.

These parasites can live in your gut for over 25 years and grow rapidly.

Did you know a **82-foot-long** tapeworm was once removed from a patient in India? Way to go!

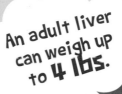

82 feet

FILTHY FLUIDS

It pays to stay in tip-top condition!

AAAATCHOO!

When we sneeze, snot shoots out at **100 mph**, traveling up to **26 feet**—that's half the length of a bowling alley!

26 feet

SLIME MACHINE

Snot is mucus, a gunky slime that stops germs from getting into our lungs and lubricates our insides.

BOOGER TIME!

You produce over a quart of mucus every single day. That's **100 gallons** of boogers each year!

WHAT IS SPIT?

On average, humans produce half a gallon of saliva *per day*.

It's 99 percent water, but the remaining 1 per cent is a concoction of mucus, enzymes to help digest food, and antimicrobial agents.

In a person's lifetime, they will produce enough saliva to fill up **two swimming pools!**

Before you go "swapping spit" with someone, scientists found that a **10 second** kiss can transfer over **80 billion** types of bacteria! Yuck!

SWEAT ON!

The average human being sweats over 264 gallons each year—a whole jacuzzi load!

Your feet alone have over **250,000** sweat glands. More than any other part of your body.

PICK 'N' FLICK

It's tempting to pick at things, especially if you're fidgety!

TOUGH SHIELD
A scab protects the skin while it heals underneath.

WHAT IS A SCAB?

Scaly scabs are tempting to pick, but it's best to leave well alone, even if they're itchy!

When you cut yourself, special blood cells called platelets form a clot to protect the wound.

The platelets make a net of fibers that trap red blood cells to form a scab.

DID YOU KNOW?
Long ago, ear wax was recommended as a lip balm. Tasty!

EAR-EAR!

Ear wax is a mixture of dead skin cells and bodily fluids that helps to collect dirt and debris.

In fact, the chemicals in ear wax can help to fight infection and keep your ear canals moist.

GUNKY FIGHT

When your body fights infection, white blood cells rush to the scene. You may notice a gungy gloop in this area called pus.

Pus is made from dead white blood cells and bacteria.

Depending on the infection you're facing, it could be yellow, brown, green, or white.

WHAT IS A PIMPLE?

A pimple is pus on the surface of the skin, but be careful not to pop it, as you could introduce more bacteria! And more bacteria can only lead to more pus . . .

SHEDDING SKIN

Did you know that you shed your outer layer of skin every two to four weeks—about 30,000–40,000 skin cells a minute?

You shed about **9 lbs** of skin a year, or the weight of **6.5 basketballs!**

Sometimes a virus in the skin can cause a clumpy knob of cells called a wart.

VILE VOMIT

Being sick is no joke, but trust your body's instinct!

PROTECTIVE PUKE

No one likes to barf, but it's your body's way of protecting you.

Throwing up gets rid of harmful substances or something that's irritating your gut. It's a simple, quick exit strategy!

Vomit contains half-digested food mixed with saliva, stomach lining, and digestive juices. No wonder it smells so cheesy.

GO WITH THE FLOW

WAY TO GO!

When you vomit, muscles in your stomach and intestines push your food up instead of down.

Some vomits are record-breakers. Projectile vomit comes out with such a force that droplets can travel up to 26 feet.

Projectile vomit can travel four times the length of a bed! Get the umbrellas out!

26 feet

BURNING BARF

Your digestive juices are so acidic they could wreck your teeth!

This is why your body produces more saliva when you vomit, to dilute it.

Frequent vomiting can also lead to dehydration, so see a doctor if you're barfing too much.

OPEN WIDE!
Be grateful you're not a penguin chick—your mother would feed you with her vomit!

Vomit can be a sign of illness or excess.

Germs may be lurking in your digestive system, or perhaps you've guzzled too much food.

Stress and anxiety can make you feel queasy, just like spinning too fast at a carnival! But trust your body and go with it. Just keep your hair out of the way...

AWFUL ANIMALS

From slimy slugs and fearsome fish to filthy flies and pesky parasites, it's time to explore some stinky scavengers, nose-pickers, poop-flickers, and devilish dinosaurs.

page 28

AWFUL
AMPHIBIANS

ROTTEN
REPTILES

page 30

page 32

GROSS
HABITS

page 34

DISGUSTING
DINOSAURS

WORMS AND JELLIES

If it feels a bit squishy, it's probably best avoided!

SLUGS AND SNAILS

Slugs and snails are gastropods, which means "stomach foot." This is because they use their entire bodies to move around.

Slugs breathe through a blowhole from the side of their bodies. They can also stretch to 20 times their length!

Slug slime is thicker than a snail's, but an angry snail's slime is extra foamy! Both are used to help them "ripple" along with ease.

Snail slime is used in some face care treatments for extra smooth skin.

DID YOU KNOW?
Slugs have **27,000** teeth—that's more teeth than a shark!

BONE-EATING SNOT FLOWER WORM

AKA *Osedax Mucofloris*, this worm's entire existence consists of drilling into the bones of dead whales on the seabed to feed on tissue and fatty acids inside.

These worms have no mouth or teeth, instead using acid to tunnel into the bones.

FEASTING FISH

Hagfish are a gunky force to be reckoned with! If attacked, they spit out up to a quart of goo so thick that it can suffocate their predators.

They eat worms mostly, but also scavenge dead or dying fish, tearing into carcasses with four sets of sharp, comb-shaped teeth along their tongue.

The largest known hagfish measured **4 ft 2 in** long!

4 ft 2 in

GRIM PICKINGS!
Hagfish even swim inside the dead fish to eat it from the inside out.

MISCHIEF MAGGOTS

Maggots follow one rule: if it's rotting, it's dinner!

They're even used in some medical treatments of non-healing wounds. They nibble away at the dead tissue while leaving the live stuff untouched.

CREEPIN' AND CRAWLIN'

Pesky visitors that are rarely welcome!

Houseflies taste with their feet. They love the sweat and salt on your skin!

SWATS AWAY

Beware the pesky housefly that lands on your food.

Houseflies can't eat solids, so they spit and vomit on their food to liquefy it—then suck it up. Nice!

They also lay their eggs on dead flesh and like to eat poop. Their manners leave a lot to be desired.

GRUESOME GUEST!
Flies poop every few minutes and carry about two million bacteria. Not the most welcome of visitors!

SUPER SUCKERS

All spiders inject their prey with venom that liquefies their flesh, which they then suck up.

The goliath bird-eating spider is a type of tarantula, and one of the world's largest spiders.

It makes a tasty meal (or shake) of lizards, bats, and even snakes!

SUPERSIZED SPIDER
It grows up to 6 in long and has jaws the size of a cheetah's claws.

PLAYING HOST

Parasites are crafty creatures that live on (or in) a host organism to get their food.

Whale sharks have to swim along while they poop, in case parasites swim up their bottoms!

It's fair to say that fish would rather not meet the tongue-eating louse. This creature creeps through a fish's gills, eats the tongue, and then becomes the tongue! It spends the rest of its life feeding off the fish. How rude!

TOUGH COOKIES

Cockroaches are the tough guys of the critter world—if you cut off their head, they'll still survive for a week!

A headless cockroach breathes through holes in its body segments, but will eventually die from thirst.

The world's largest cockroach is 6 in long, which is as long as an adult hand! It also has a 12 in wingspan. It's found in South America, in case you were wondering.

6 inches

'ello!

STOMACH-CHURNING SEA CREATURES

Sometimes it's the quiet ones you have to watch ...

Sea cucumbers breathe water in and out through their butt!

BOTTOMS UP

Sea cucumbers look harmless enough, but if you get too close, they'll shoot their sticky intestines out from their butt!

This stuns potential predators, giving the sea cucumber time to escape.

Some lampreys use their teeth to scrape algae from rocks.

FREAKY FACT!
If a predator starts gobbling a sea cucumber's guts, the cucumber just grows them back again.

STAR TURN

Starfish have a tiny mouth, but this doesn't deter them from eating a mammoth meal!

They simply push their stomach out through their mouth to cover and digest their prey.

CORAL CRUNCHER
The crown of thorns starfish is covered with venomous spines, and it likes nothing better than munching on rock-hard coral polyps.

Yum, yum!

TOUGH COMPETITION

Baby gray nurse sharks have a hard time from the day they're born.

If they're not the first to hatch from their eggs, they're in danger of being eaten by their brother or sister who hatched first. Talk about sibling rivalry!

VAMPIRE BITE

Lampreys, or "vampire fish," are one of the strangest looking sea creatures, with a jawless mouth, and twelve circular rows of sharp teeth.

They use their suction-cup mouth to bore holes in the flesh of unsuspecting prey and suck their blood, while some species also feast on the flesh.

AWFUL AMPHIBIANS

Instead of being sick, a frog throws up its entire stomach, then cleans it with its hands, and swallows it back down again.

Gross!

Some rude habits really take the cake . . .

THAT'S SICK!

Frogs look cute with their googly eyes, but they have some disgusting habits!

GORY FACT ALERT!
A frog also sheds its skin regularly, and usually eats it!

SKIN TO SKIN

What about the Surinam toad, who lets her incubating babies embed themselves in the skin of her back?

When the toad's offspring are fully formed, they burst out and swim away, tearing holes in her flesh. Talk about being taken for granted!

SLIMY FEAST

Baby caecilians also take liberties by feeding on their mother's skin.

These worm-like creatures sit within their mother's coils and feed on the "skin sap"—nutrient-filled secretions and mucus.

IN COLD BLOOD

Salamanders look a bit like a frog crossed with a lizard. They feast on worms, slugs, and snails, but some species even feast on each other!

They do this when they're hungry, but also to remove competition when resources are scarce.

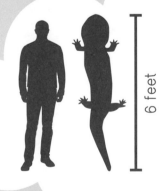

6 feet

The Chinese giant salamander is the largest amphibian on the planet! It can grow up to **6 feet long!**

ROTTEN REPTILES

These bad boys have some peculiar traits . . .

DID YOU KNOW?
Crocodiles replace each of their teeth up to **50** times during their lifetime.

PEARLY WHITES

Crocodiles regularly lose their teeth, but there's always some ready to replace them.

It's no surprise the teeth fall out regularly . . .

. . . they swallow small stones to help grind and digest their food!

Their stomachs are also extremely acidic, helping to dissolve and digest bones, hooves, horns, and shells.

BAD BLOOD

You don't want to mess with a horned lizard!

If it feels threatened, it'll squirt you with blood from its eyes. Horned lizards usually aim for their aggressor's mouth because their blood is said to taste so foul.

The horned lizard is a powerful shot too, squirting blood up to 3 feet—that's longer than an adult's arm.

3 feet

FROM TOP TO TOE

Fitzroy River turtles have a rigid shell, making it difficult to expand their chest to breathe, so instead they've adapted to breathe through their bottom (cloaca).

Chinese softshell turtles also pee through their mouth! When they get a chance, they dip their head into a puddle to rinse the urine away.

This mouthwash isn't very refreshing!

FREAKY FACT!
A python can open its mouth four times wider than its skull.

BIG GULP

Ever been told to chew your food properly before you swallow? Try telling that to a python.

These huge snakes have been known to eat an antelope whole!

To prepare its feast, the python wraps itself tightly around its prey to suffocate it before swallowing the meal in one go. Such a mammoth meal will take weeks to digest!

31

GROSS HABITS

Poop, snot, and vomit! What's not to like?

FULL OF FECES

We all like a party trick, but some animals take it too far!

Hippopotamuses try to impress their female friends by pooping and spinning their tails to fling their poop around.

DID YOU KNOW?
Wombats arrange their cube-shaped poop into small piles to mark their territory.

COOL IT!

We've all wanted to turn on the sprinkler or take a cool shower, but turkey vultures have a stinky solution on hot days—they just pee or poop down their legs.

What's more, if a turkey vulture is attacked, it'll vomit in the face of the aggressor. That's a way of saying "don't mess with me."

QUICK PICK

Many people admit to picking their nose, and animals are no exception!

Found in the forests of Madagascar, the aye-aye has been spotted having a crafty pick with its 3-inch-long finger almost entirely up its nose, before licking it clean.

In fact, an aye-aye's finger could reach almost to the back of its throat. Now, that's dedication for you!

ACTUAL SIZE!

3 inches

TRASH TALKERS

Fulmar chicks are a dab hand at projectile vomiting.

If they feel threatened by other birds, they'll throw up an oily fluid that smells like rotten fish. The oil can stick the aggressor's feathers together, making it difficult to fly away.

Stand back! I'm loaded!

Watch out for llamas. They'll spit if they don't like you and it's full of food fragments from their stomach—a bit stinky!

DISGUSTING DINOSAURS

Let's scale-up the size of all things gross.

BIG ITCH

Some dinosaurs were the largest creatures to ever walk on the planet—even their parasites were supersized!

Dinosaurs played host to blood-sucking fleas. They didn't really have the hands to swat them away, so they just had to put up with it!

Dino fleas could be **1 inch long**—that's about **10 times** the size of a modern flea!

Argh! I can't scratch with these short arms!

CRAZY CANNIBAL

When food was scarce, the *tyrannosaurus rex* resorted to eating each other.

Serrated tooth marks on T. rex bones are a sign that no other large predator could have been the aggressor.

A T. rex tooth could be more than **8 inches long**— about two-thirds the length of an adult foot!

8 inches

OUT BOTH ENDS

Dinosaurs were prone to puking, too.

In 2002, the fossilized vomit of an ichthyosaur was found in the UK and thought to be 160 million years old.

TISSUE ALERT!

When you're talking size, dinosaur snot is award-winning too.

Scientists discovered the huge sinus cavities of the T. rex would have held over 8 gallons of snot. That would make a sneeze one mighty rain shower!

A T. rex could have filled a bath tub in just five sneezes!

Fossilized dino poop is called a coprolite.

When some dinosaurs pooped, they dumped up to **5 gallons of poop** at a time. The saving grace was their feces made the ground very fertile.

SICKENING SOCIETY

From what we do in secret to what we do for medals, here are some of the weirdest and downright dirtiest ways we humans live our lives!

HORRIBLE HABITS

page 40

page 42

ICKY TOURISM

GROSS RECORDS!

Some people will stop at nothing to get into the record books.

YUCK! Ken Edwards ate **36** cockroaches in less than a minute.

Colin Shirlow swallowed **233** oysters in three minutes.

GULLET GAMES

Check out these bizarre eating challenges!

Takeru Kobayashi ate **57** cow brains in **15** minutes. It's a wonder what people will do next!

CRAZY HANDS

The world's longest nails have a combined length of over 43 feet, which is longer than a school bus!

And they've taken decades to grow— Diana Armstrong last cut her nails in 1997.

The longest is the right thumbnail, at nearly 4.6 ft.

MILK SNEEZE

One of the world's most bizarre records is held by Ilker Yilmaz from Turkey. In 2004, he squirted milk from his eyes nearly 9 feet across a room!

9 feet

Ilker snorted the milk up into his nose, and then squirted it out of his left eye.

If they're ever painted, it takes up to **20** bottles of nail polish.

TONGUE-TASTIC!

The heaviest weight lifted by a human tongue is 28.5 lbs, or over five bags of sugar.

Thomas Blackthorne, from the UK, lifted the weight with a hook that pierced right through his tongue!

4.6 feet

HORRIBLE HABITS

Hands up if you have a dirty secret? Will you dare to bare the truth?

BATHROOM ANTICS

We all have habits we keep secret, but some of these are off the scale!

Let's take the bathroom: peeing in the shower, refusing to wash our hands after using the toilet, or using someone else's toothbrush. Can you beat that?

NO ONE'S LOOKING

In the bedroom, too, unwashed bed sheets, laundry on the floor, moldy mugs of coffee, and flicking boogers.

Perhaps you've smelled the pus after you've squeezed a zit (best stop there!).

QUICK AS A FLASH

The "five second rule" is useful if you drop your favorite snack, but sadly it's not true.

Scientists have found that bacteria can attach themselves to food as soon as it hits the floor, particularly if surfaces are wet.

CRAFTY SNIP

Toenail clippings are a contentious issue.

Perhaps you've found them on the floor, in the bed, on the sofa, or even on the kitchen table!

FREAKY FACT!
Some people even admit to biting their toenails. That takes a bit of perseverance!

ICKY TOURISM

Tired of art galleries or impressive buildings? It's time to discover these beauties.

Today's gum wall is covered with the chewed leftovers of thousands of pieces of gum!

STICK 'EM UP!

If you visit the Pike Place Market in Seattle, USA, you'll find a gum wall over 50 feet long!

In 1993, theater visitors began sticking their chewing gum to the wall as they waited for a show.

GUM ART?
Some pieces of gum have been stuck impressively high, and others have formed little sculptures.

LOCKS AWAY

If you visit the basement of a ceramics shop in Avanos, Turkey, you'll be surprised to find hair samples from around the world.

This pop-up museum began when a potter's female friend was moving away and gave him a lock of her hair for remembrance.

Other women began to follow this tradition and, within 40 years, an impressive collection had grown.

HAIR-RAISING!
The museum has hair samples from over 16,000 women!

MUCKY MACHINE

Another challenging visit is the Museum of Old and New Art (MONA) in Tasmania, Australia, where you'll find the Cloaca machine that's full of feces!

The machine's whirring tubes and bags replicate the workings of our digestive system. It's given food and produces poop—simple as that.

FOOD FANTASIES

In Malmö, Sweden, the Disgusting Food Museum isn't for the squeamish.

It features 80 of the world's most disgusting foods, with the opportunity to smell and taste a few. You might not want to go there on an empty stomach.

STINKY CHEESE! The museum features Casu Marzu, a sheep milk cheese that contains live maggots! Bon appétit!

MODERN MEDICINE

It's mind-blowing what medicine can do for us—but take a deep breath!

KNEE OR ANKLE?

Doctors can do amazing things and these days we have a lot to be thankful for. Like rotationplasty!

This extraordinary surgery can turn an ankle into a knee joint. The procedure is usually performed when a child has their leg amputated after a bone tumor.

Attaching the child's foot to their knee "backward" creates a new knee joint, which can be fitted with a prosthetic leg.

HEAD TURNING

Scientists think it may be possible to treat paralyzed patients by transplanting their head onto a new body.

So far, the procedure has been carried out on a corpse, but scientists think it may be possible with a live body by 2030.

The head and body would be cooled to stop blood circulation and brain function, and to reduce nerve damage.

. . . Err? What just happened?

TOOTH-TASTIC!

You wouldn't believe it, but doctors can use a tooth to restore sight.

During the procedure, doctors extract a tooth, drill a hole in it, and insert a plastic lens. The tooth is then implanted in the patient's cheek where it grows new blood vessels, before being implanted into the eye.

BRAIN POWER

It's an extreme measure, but a hemispherectomy can be a lifesaver for children who suffer from seizures.

By removing the part of the brain that causes the seizures the remaining part can usually compensate for some brain functions.

A hemispherectomy can take up to 12 hours to complete.

SPACE TRAVEL

You need a head for heights to navigate space, and an open mind, too!

WASH BAG

Astronauts pack a toothbrush when they go into space, but they clean their teeth in a different way.

With no running water in space, they use a water pouch to wet their brush before adding normal toothpaste.

Astronauts have to swallow after they brush their teeth because there's nowhere to spit out.

KEEP IT DOWN

It's difficult to navigate zero-gravity.

You can't burp in space, because the gas is mixed with your food and liquid, so they come up, too!

WATER WORKS

With no running water, astronauts wash their hands and body with a cloth and a no-rinse soap.

There's no water for washing clothes either, so astronauts wear their clothes until they need throwing away. Stinky!

If astronauts are out and about on a spacewalk, special diapers take care of everything.

Astronauts pee into a tube which gets sucked into a bin. The urine is then purified back into their drinking water!

They also poop in a special bag which is freeze-dried and stored.

This contraption is the toilet on the International Space Station. Its catchy name is the Universal Waste Management System.

DIZZY SPELL

Space travel is a big deal, and nearly half of astronauts suffer from "space sickness." No one wants to vomit in space—it's hard to contain it!

Space travel can be disorienting. When you tilt your head on Earth, parts of your ears send signals to your brain, but in space, these signals aren't activated.

WORRYING WASTE

If you've grown used to a throwaway culture, you may want to think again.

LANDFILL LIFE

Next time you reach for a trash can, think before you throw your waste away. Landfill sites are full of trash that takes years to degrade:

Tin can: **50 years**

Wool clothing: **Up to 5 years**

"Disposable" diaper: **Up to 500 years**

TOXIC MIX

Be careful if you visit an abandoned chemical factory in Ranipet, India.

The factory used to supply chemicals for the leather industry, but was abandoned in the 1990s. Since then, chromium sludge has seeped into the groundwater, causing a health hazard for nearby residents.

You'll find **2.75 million tons** of toxic waste piled about **16 feet** tall!

DANGEROUS DUMP

When rainfall seeps through the junk in a landfill site, a contaminated liquid called leachate is produced, which can pollute nearby land and water sources.

METHANE MENACE!
Rotting landfill waste also releases methane, a greenhouse gas that's **25 times** more potent than carbon dioxide.

Cigarette butt: **12 years**

Plastic waste: **up to 1,000 years**

SEWAGE SLUDGE

...horrible humans!

Every day, millions of gallons of raw sewage flows into the Ganges River in India and Bangladesh—even though the river is a vital source of water for washing and drinking.

Even an orange peel takes **6 months!**

Raw sewage is also found on the streets of Maputo, Mozambique, because the sewage system there only covers a small part of the city.

HORRENDOUS HISTORY

Thank your lucky stars you're not living in the Dark Ages. Our ancestors were faced with all kinds of horrors: petrifying punishments, dangerous dentistry, filthy fashions, and foul food. As we turn back the clock, keep hold of your stomach. You're in for a yucky ride!

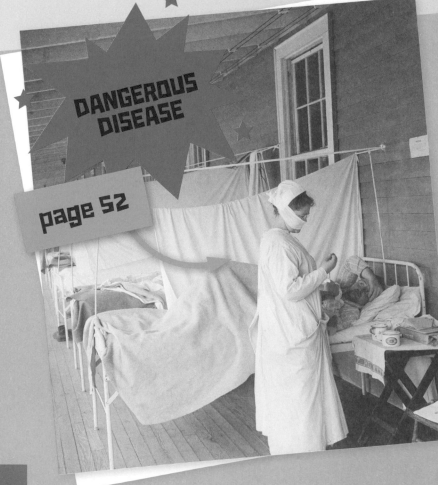

DANGEROUS DISEASE

page 52

page 54

MASHUP MEDICINE

DANGEROUS DISEASE

Without modern medicine, infection was a matter of life or death.

DID YOU KNOW?
The Black Death killed up to **200** million people.

Black Death doctors wore this scary mask which they believed protected them from the plague!

BLACK DEATH

In the 14th century, a terrible plague swept through Europe, Asia, and North Africa.

Victims of the Black Death had a ferocious fever, as well as vomiting, painful swellings, and blotchy skin.

The plague bacterium was spread by flea-infested rats that were carried around on merchant ships.

FEARSOME FLU

25 MILLION: The number of people the flu outbreak killed in the first six months.

Between 1918 and 1920, a terrible flu infected over a third of the world's population.

This flu pandemic was particularly fearsome because it affected healthy young adults, not just those with a weakened immune system, and it spread rapidly.

DEADLY DISEASE! Up to 50 million people died—that's more deaths than in the First World War (1914-1918).

FLESH EATER

Did you know there's a rare skin infection that can cause a flesh-eating disease?

First identified in the 5th century BCE, this condition can be deadly if it's not treated quickly. The bacteria are thought to enter the body through a wound, burn, or bite.

ACRID AMMUNITION

In the Middle Ages, disease was used as a weapon of war.

During a siege, sneaky soldiers would spread infection by catapulting dead animals or rotting corpses over castle walls. It would be difficult for those inside to get rid of the stinking, rotting flesh.

MASHUP MEDICINE

These ancient treatments might make your skin crawl.

I need this like a hole in the head!

STRANGE THEORIES

BLOOD SUCKERS!
Leeches suck up to ten times their own body weight in blood per feed.

In ancient times, bloodletting (removing "bad" blood) was a medical practice thought to cure disease. Doctors would drain blood from a vein or use leeches.

Another painful procedure was drilling a hole in the skull. Called trepanning, it was thought to relieve head injuries, pain, or to remove "evil spirits."

ABOVE AND BEYOND

Some doctors have gone to extreme measures to understand disease.

In the 18th century, US doctor Stubbins Ffirth drank yellow-fever-infected vomit to see how the disease spread (even though mosquitoes were to blame).

And in the 19th century, Giovanni Grassi ate roundworm eggs from a dead man's body to prove how they were transmitted. The eggs later hatched in his own poop!

ANIMAL AID

The ancient Greeks treated wounds with slugs or snails that had been boiled and crushed.

For bad eyesight, the ancient Egyptians recommended rubbing your eyes with mashed tortoise brains.

In the 17th century, chicken poop was thought to cure baldness—if you could stand the stench!

SHOCKING STUFF!
The ancient Greeks used the shocks from electric ray fish to treat headaches and arthritis.

Nice!

DIRE DENTISTRY

GORY FACT ALERT!
In Tudor times, dentists used a poop and honey mix to make rotten teeth fall out.

After the Battle of Waterloo in 1815, scavengers took the teeth of dead soldiers, and these "Waterloo Teeth" were later sold to make dentures.

The Romans used crushed mouse brains as a toothpaste, as well as urine for a mouthwash.

Gulp!

55

HARSH PUNISHMENT

It's tough to be fined or imprisoned, but spare a thought for these criminals . . .

LESSONS LEARNED

DINNER TIME!
Under some emperors of ancient Rome, a condemned person was simply thrown to the lions.

In some parts of Asia, particularly India, serious crimes were punished by execution by elephant! This usually involved an elephant trampling on a victim, and pressing on their head or tummy with a foot.

LIQUID LAMENT

Some ancient forms of punishment saw prisoners forced to drink scalding molten metal. Not surprisingly, this caused severe internal damage.

Others were sprinkled with boiling oil, water, tar, or acid.

DID YOU KNOW?
Criminals found guilty of treason were "hung," "drawn," (organs removed while still alive) and "quartered" (body cut into pieces). It was simply to say, don't mess with the law!

TERRIBLE TREATMENTS

In Europe in the Middle Ages, it wasn't unusual for a criminal to be boiled or skinned alive or to have their body stretched on a rack.

If you were given the "breaking wheel," you were tied to a wooden wheel while an iron bar was used to break your bones, and then left to bleed to death.

PIRATE PUNISHMENT

Pirates were no pushovers either. They flogged their crew using a knotted whip called a "cat o' nine tails" that would tear a victim's skin.

Cat o' nine tails

OUCH!
"Keelhauling" saw sailors stripped and dragged beneath the boat's hull, where they would inevitably drown.

A DAY IN THE LIFE

It's a wonder civilization ever developed at all!

STINKY!
Louis XIV of France said he only took **three baths** in his lifetime.

What's that terrible smell?

AN OLD SOAK

In the Middle Ages, people rarely took a bath. They thought immersing themselves in water might bring the risk of disease, and were prudish about getting naked.

PHEW!
But Queen Isabella of Castile wins the stinky prize. She boasted that she only took **two baths** in her lifetime—one on the day she was born, and one on her wedding night.

TOILET TROUBLE

Before toilet paper was invented, the ancient Romans used a sponge on a stick, which was then soaked in saltwater ready for the next person.

Later, rich people used wool or lace, while the poor used rags, or leaves.

Can nobody use a handkerchief?

FREAKY FACT!
The Romans would also pee into pots, which were left out to be collected. The local laundry service used urine to wash clothes!

SNOTS AWAY

The ancient Greeks and Romans thought sneezing was a good omen—unless you sneezed too many times.

Some ancient cultures believed a sneeze was a way of being freed from an evil spirit.

DID YOU KNOW?
French leader Napoleon Bonaparte had brass buttons added to the sleeves of military uniforms. He wanted to stop his soldiers wiping their mouths and noses there.

Romans considered dormice a delicacy. No wonder they wanted to vomit!

CHEERS!

In ancient Rome, a "sports drink" made from powdered goat dung and vinegar was popular with chariot racers.

When the Romans had a dinner party, they went to great lengths to impress their guests. It was quite normal for visitors to make themselves puke so they had room to gorge some more.

STOMACH-TURNING TRENDS

It takes dedication to look this good . . .

FREAKY FACT!
Elizabeth I used poisonous white lead makeup to keep her complexion as pale as possible!

DRASTIC MEASURES

You may think having a tan looks good, but in the Middle Ages, pale skin was all the rage.

While women (Lizzy included) didn't realize lead was poisonous at the time, they would also put leeches on their skin to suck their blood to achieve a pale pigmentation.

SWEET AROMA

The ancient Egyptians liked to wear perfume, but in the strangest way.

They wore cone "hats" of resin or ox fat infused with aromatic oils.

The cones gradually melted, coating the Egyptians in a fragrant oil. They probably got a bit sticky as well!

TOP NOTCH

Hair treatments were also popular throughout history.

For a sensational blond look, the ancient Romans used a hair dye of pigeon poop.

In the 18th century, wigs were all the rage—and the bigger the better. Animal lard was often used to hold the wigs in place, but unfortunately the lard attracted lice—and the occasional rat!

BEAUTIFUL BROWS

The ancient Greeks loved a good brow. In fact, the thicker the better! It was said to be a sign of beauty and brains.

Greek women would use kohl or soot to line their brows, while others used tree resin to stick goat hair to their forehead!

HAIR-RAISING!
Wigs in the 18th century were big and ornate, and decorated with jewels, and even model boats!

ANCIENT EATS

You may need to hold your nose for these digestive delights.

BLEGH!
As the warmth of the sun caused the fish to ferment, the guts would break down into a thick liquid.

FOUL FISH

In ancient Greece and Rome, a rancid fish sauce called garum was considered a delicacy.

Garum was made by mixing brine and herbs with fish intestines and blood, and then leaving it to rot for several months.

PLUMP AND JUICY

The ancient Roman elite didn't stop with stuffed dormice.

While they would gut the creatures and fill them with ground pork before baking in an oven. Other curious delicacies of the time included flamingo tongues and pig's wombs.

Wouldn't you prefer a nice, plump dormouse?

JELLY-TASTIC

In Victorian times, savory jellies were all the rage.

It was common to make a gelatin from calves' feet. The feet were boiled to extract the natural gelatin, mixed with sugar or spices, and then cooled to set.

Beef was also boiled in water and salt to make beef tea.

GET STUFFED

Today, turducken is an elaborate dish in which a deboned chicken is stuffed inside a deboned duck and then stuffed inside a deboned turkey.

But in 1807, a chef went one step further by stuffing 17 birds inside each other. That calls for a big appetite!

I'm not going in there!

FULL TO THE BRIM!
Can you imagine eating a warbler, a bunting, a lark, a thrush, a quail, a lapwing, a plover, a partridge, a woodcock, a teal, a guinea fowl, a duck, a chicken, a pheasant, a goose, a turkey, and a great bustard?

KEEPING MEMORIES ALIVE

For many cultures, death wasn't the end of everything, but the start of some new adventure!

DID YOU KNOW? The mummification process took **70 days.**

The body was left to dry out and then wrapped in strips of linen.

The oldest Egyptian mummies are thought to be about **8,000** years old.

EVERLASTING

The ancient Egyptian ritual of mummification preserved a body so it could be transported to the afterlife.

The heart was left untouched, but other organs were extracted, and the brain was removed through the nostrils with a special hook.

BACK TO LIFE?

Cryogenic freezing is the process of freezing cells, tissues, organs, or even entire bodies to protect them from decay.

They are frozen in the hope that they can be brought back to life in the future, when science has developed a way to revive, and perhaps even cure them.

CHILLY!
The process takes place over several days to minimize damage, until the body has reached -328 °F.

FACIAL FEATURES

The Egyptians used to bury a death mask with a person to help their spirit find their body in the afterlife.

The masks were made by taking a cast or impression from a corpse. In later years, death masks were simply used for remembrance.

This death mask was made of the French emperor Napoleon Bonaparte.

Can I move yet?

LASTING IMAGE

In Victorian Britain, death photography was a way of honoring the dead.

It seems morbid, but at the time, it was a way to create precious memories—although cozying up to a corpse wasn't the most hygienic thing to do.

A nice family portrait. But one of them could be dead!

NAUSEOUS NATURE

Our natural world is a marvel, but it's not for the fainthearted! There's creepy caves and reeking rainforests. There's sewage-filled seas and filthy fungi—even your household is full of horrors! Take a look at your natural surroundings, if you dare.

page 70

STRONG STENCH

page 68

CURIOUS CAVERNS

CURIOUS CAVERNS

Would you delve deep underground if you knew what lay beneath?

HOME TO ROOST

Deep in the rainforests of Borneo, the Mulu Caves are a popular tourist attraction.

They come alive at dusk with a flurry of wings as swifts and swallows fly home to roost, and bats fly out.

FREAKY FACT!

The caves are also home to swiftlet bird's nests, which are used for the Chinese delicacy "bird's nest soup." These nests are made purely from bird spit!

SPIDER ALERT

Wind Cave in South Dakota, USA, may not have resident creatures, but you'd be forgiven for feeling a little scared.

The caves have formed a honeycomb-like structure of "boxwork" calcite, which looks like a scary giant spider's web.

BIT BATTY

The Gomantong Caves in Borneo are also home to some fearsome nighttime creatures, from bats and rats to cockroaches, spiders, and giant centipedes.

In fact, about 2 million bats sleep in the caves by day.

Do you know where the toilet is?

POOO-EY!
Not surprisingly, the cave floor is covered with centuries-old bat poop—it's rather stinky!

ROTTEN REMAINS

Deep beneath the city streets of Paris lie the bones of the dead.

The Paris catacombs were originally dug out in the 13th century as a source of limestone to build the city.

BURYING BONES
By the 18th century, the city's cemeteries were overflowing and the empty tunnels seemed the best place to transfer the remains.

The catacombs are said to hold the remains of 6–7 million dead Parisians!

69

STRONG STENCH

It's a stinky old world out there . . .

REEKING RAINFORESTS

You won't miss the carrion flower (or corpse flower) because it reeks of rotting flesh!

Found in the rainforests of Borneo and Sumatra, some species also have the smell of blood, urine, and poop.

Some only bloom for a short time, so they need to attract pollinators fast. Their stench attracts flies, beetles, and other insects.

Some of the flowers have a bowl-like structure which traps insects inside, long enough for them to help pollinate it.

Get a whiff of this!

SURVIVAL SPRAY

When skunks feel threatened, they shoot a stinky spray from their anal glands.

It can travel 10 feet and be detected over a mile away!

THIS WAY TO THE STINK!

The skunk's stripes point toward the scene of the crime—perhaps to deter predators without having to use precious ammunition.

SKUNK CABBAGE

The skunk cabbage grows in swampy conditions.

As its name suggests, it gives off a smell of skunk (or rotting meat) when it blooms or its leaves are crushed. This attracts the same unusual pollinators as the corpse flower.

WHAT A STINK!

When a hoatzin belches, it smells of cow manure!

Skunk cabbages have an amazing ability to heat up when they're flowering. This helps them to bloom in icy conditions and even to melt the surrounding snow.

BAD BREATH

Hoatzin are a species of tropical bird found in South America.

Their leafy diet is difficult to digest so, like cows, their food ferments in their gut and produces stinky methane.

SEWAGE SWIM

It's a sad fact, but 80 percent of the world's sewage finds its way into the oceans, untreated

When sewage systems become overwhelmed, sewage and gray water (from laundry, sinks, and showers) is sometimes released into rivers and oceans.

WASTE AT SEA

Our oceans have become a dumping ground . . .

PLASTIC PILEUP

Disgusting!

Some plastic debris floats on the surface of the oceans, while around 70 percent sinks.

Synthetic clothes contain tiny fibers (from fabrics such as polyester and nylon) that are less than a quarter of an inch long. These microfibers can't be filtered by water treatment plants and find their way into fish and plankton.

Our oceans are thought to contain over **5 trillion** pieces of plastic.

Every week, a large cruise ship releases **over 158,000 gallons** of sewage into the water!

COASTAL CLEAN-UP

Worryingly, some sewage traces are impossible to see. Authorities do regular tests to ensure that beaches are clean.

At the shoreline, one milliliter of ocean water contains **about 10 million viruses!** But thankfully, most aren't harmful to humans. In the open sea, viruses are less concentrated.

1 ml ▶

x 10,000,000

LOAD OF GARBAGE

The Great Pacific Garbage Patch is the world's largest collection of ocean plastic.

Found in the middle of the Pacific, circular ocean currents make it difficult for the debris to escape.

Every major ocean has a garbage patch and almost half are made up of abandoned or lost fishing nets, known as "ghost gear."

The Great Pacific Garbage Patch

DID YOU KNOW?
The Great Pacific Garbage Patch covers about **620,000 square miles** —an area three times the size of France!

GORY GROWINGS-ON

Nature is full of surprises. Be careful where you tread!

STINKY LEGS!
The octopus stinkhorn (or "devil's fingers fungus") has bright red tentacles up to 3 inches long that splay out like an octopus' legs.

Flies are attracted to the stinky smell and get covered in gloop before they fly away, helping to spread the spores. You can often smell a stinkhorn before you see it!

FILTHY FUNGI

Stinkhorn mushrooms reek of rotting flesh!

Help!

These fungi grow from a type of squishy "egg" found submerged in the soil and ooze a sticky, gloopy liquid full of spores.

DEVIL'S TEETH

Deep in the forests of Europe and North America, beware the bleeding tooth (or "devil's tooth") fungus.

Thankfully, they won't bite! But they do have a vampire-like appearance, with bright red globules that seem to "bleed" from their flesh.

Another terrible sight is the purple "jellydisc fungus," which could be mistaken for intestines splattered on the forest floor!

MEAT STEW

Carnivorous plants are crafty hunters. They attract, trap, and digest their prey—from tiny insects to reptiles and small mammals.

Some use brightly colored leaves and nectar to lure unsuspecting victims, while others are cleverly camouflaged.

CRAFTY CATCH

Pitcher plants are the world's largest carnivorous plants.

Their urn-shaped traps can catch small mammals, and some even feast on whole rats!

Small mammals are attracted by the bright colors and sweet nectar, then fall in and drown in digestive juices.

Dinner's ready!

SNAP!
Venus flytrap plants catch flies in their trapdoor leaves, dissolve their prey and absorb the nutritious stew they've created!

HOUSEHOLD HORRORS

Your home may look sparkling clean, but beware of invisible invaders.

129,000 bacteria per square inch.

STINKY SINKS

Did you know, your kitchen or bathroom sink probably has more bacteria than your toilet!

If your kitchen cloth begins to whiff, it's because it has millions of bacteria growing on it. Time to replace!

Over 120 bacteria per square inch.

DID YOU KNOW?

Scientists have calculated about **129,000 bacteria per square inch** in a bathroom sink, compared to just **120 per square inch** on a toilet seat.

TV remote controls carry up to 20 times more bacteria than your toilet seat!

DEEP CLEAN

Other items in your home can attract a horde of bacteria.

Mobile phones are a dirty culprit too, and even a desk can carry over 19,000 bacteria per square inch.

Biting your nails or chewing a pen are also a no-no—especially if someone else has chewed the pen first!

FEARSOME FLUSH

5 feet

Do you close the toilet lid before you flush? No? You might change your mind if you knew each flush sends a 5-feet cloud of bacteria into the air, especially if your toothbrush is stored close by!

When you use a public restroom, chances are the first stall is the cleanest, because it's the least used.

NOW WASH YOUR HANDS! Only **80 per cent** of people wash their hands after using the restroom, and only **30 percent** of those use soap, so beware of the door handles when you leave.

Dust mites don't bite or sting, but they can cause allergic reactions.

Up to 3 million house dust mites can live in the average bed mattress, where they feed on dead skin and hair cells.

SLEEP TIGHT?

You may be afraid of monsters under the bed, but what lies between the sheets is much scarier!

Mattresses can be a source of bacteria and viruses, too—and bed bugs if you're unlucky! It's best to vacuum and air your mattress regularly.

SURVIVING THE WILD

Some situations call for desperate measures.

BLOOD AND GUTS

Humans can survive for about three weeks without food, but only three days without water.

When Italian runner Mauro Prosperi got lost during a sandstorm in the Sahara Desert, he survived for 10 days by drinking the blood of bats.

EYE EYE!
If you find yourself stranded, you could do worse than a yak's eyeball. It's said to contain more protein than a steak!

EXTREME SHELTER

I'm always nervous when there's a bear around!

British adventurer Bear Grylls demonstrated a particularly gruesome survival technique: using a camel's carcass to keep warm.

He first removed the insides and the skin, before climbing inside for shelter and using the skin as a blanket.

POWERFUL PITS

If your mobile phone battery dies in the wild, your armpits may be able to revive it!

Put your phone in a bag and warm it under your armpit. There may be a bit of charge left when the temperature rises!

BRAVING IT

Some explorers have had to go to extreme survival measures.

When British explorer Ranulph Fiennes had frostbite, he sawed off his own fingers.

US mountaineer Aron Ralston broke his own arm and cut off his hand with a penknife to free himself from a boulder after a climbing accident.

Just hold your nose when you make the next call!

FOUL FOOD

Do you know what's really in your food or which nutritious dishes are downright disgusting? As we marvel at mold and dive into our drinks, we're in for a stomach-churning ride!

HIDDEN INGREDIENTS

page 82

MONSTROUS MOLD

page 84

HIDDEN INGREDIENTS

Food, glorious food ... if you have the taste for it.

RELAXED REGS

Our food is subject to strict safety regulations, but traces of animal feces, rat hairs, insect skin, and mold are likely to lurk in your favorite eats.

These remnants are harmless if you only eat a little. It's also too expensive for producers to take them out of the food.

Can anyone smell raspberries?

Tinned fruit is allowed to have the odd maggot, there's probably a rat hair in your chocolate, and less than half an ounce of ground oregano can have up to 1,250 insect fragments mixed in it!

NASTY SURPRISES

Our food usually goes on a long journey before we get to eat it.

It's no surprise that unusual ingredients sometimes creep in. People have reported finding frogs in cans of soda, spiders lurking among bunches of bananas, and even mice inside loaves of bread!

Check your food for any unwanted guests!

Female lac bugs secrete resin onto branches. This resin is collected and turned into shellac.

NOT-SO-SWEET TOOTH!

Sticky shellac can be found in some sugar-coated sweets. While red food coloring, or carmine, comes from boiled cochineal beetles.

UNUSUAL ADDITIVES

Did you know that raspberry flavoring (castoreum) comes from a scent gland near a beaver's bottom?

Or that L-cysteine, an ingredient in processed bread, comes from duck feathers or human hair?

Gelatin in your gummy worms is made by boiling the skin, bones, and ligaments of cows and pigs.

Carrageenan is a thickening agent that comes from seaweed. You've probably eaten it in ice cream, or in chocolate milk, because it stops the milk from separating.

MONSTROUS MOLD

Fungal spores and moldy cheese—it's a minefield out there.

HUMONGOUS FUNGUS

In the forests of Oregon, USA, you'll find the largest organism on Earth: the "honey mushroom."

Thought to be up to 8,000 years old, the fungus has spread in underground networks and moved into trees, killing them beneath their bark, and feeding on the dead wood for decades.

Some parts of the fungus are edible if they're properly cooked.

Nicknamed the "humongous fungus," the honey mushroom covers nearly **4 square miles** and weighs more than **200** blue whales!

Most of the organism spreads underground, but it also blooms above the soil to form the honey mushrooms.

GOAT-STOMACH CHEESE

You've already read about the maggot-infested Casu Marzu cheese, but how about Su Callu Sardu?

This is made from the stomach of a baby goat, full of its mother's milk.

I've got cheese inside me!

The cheese is left to mature for months, before being eaten whole (on bread or fried in lard).

NO BRAINER

Blue-brain cheese is one of the moldiest cheeses on Earth.

The cheese develops a green-blue mold and is kept at 41°F. After six months, the cheese is covered in thick black mold, and ready to eat!

BIT EGGY

If you've managed to stomach that, you might want to try this rotting delicacy.

A "century egg" is a duck, chicken, or quail's egg that's been left to rot in a mixture of clay, ash, and quicklime for months, causing the yolk to turn dark green or gray.

ROTTEN EGGS!
The rotting process gives the egg a pungent flavor, and the "white" turns into a dark brown, salty jelly. Sounds delicious!

DID YOU KNOW?
Blue-brain cheese was first made by accident. The cheesemakers left small cheese balls to mature in a damp cave . . . and forgot about them!

WORST SMELLING FOODS

Our taste and smell are closely linked. These foods take some courage!

NAT-TO YOUR LIKING?

NUTTY NATTO
Natto have a nutty flavor and are said to be extremely nutritious.

In Japan, fermented soybeans are all the rage.

Natto are sticky, gooey beans used in soup, sushi, or noodle dishes.

Their scent has been described as pungent—just like sweaty socks!

In fact, the smell is so off-putting to some people, you can now buy an "odorless" version which won't churn your stomach.

FERMENTED FISH

Did somebody say chicken?

DID YOU KNOW?
The fish is said to taste good, but is often given as a joke present to see if people can stand the challenge.

If you think cheese and rotten eggs are bad, consider fermented fish.

Surströmming is a Swedish dish made from sour, fermented herring that's been left to rot for six months.

The dish smells so bad that guidelines recommend you open the tin outdoors, although this attracts flies!

URINE FOR A TREAT

Naturally low in fat and high in protein, fried fruit bat is eaten in some parts of Asia, such as Vietnam, the Philippines, and Indonesia.

Fruit bat tastes a bit like chicken, but during the cooking process it is known to release a strong stench, like urine. Adding garlic or chili usually hides the smell.

STINKY FRUIT!
Even though it stinks, durian fruit is rich in iron, fiber, and vitamin C and is known as "king of the fruits."

KING OF THE HILL

The durian is from Southeast Asia and is also known for its vile stink that smells a bit like raw sewage and sick.

Some people love the durian fruit's nutty flavor, and it's often used in smoothies or sweet treats.

MEAT AND THEN SOME . . .

There's more to these dishes than *meats* the eye.

TRY OUR NUTRITIOUS AND DELICIOUS (?) MENU

Brain, liver, kidney, and spleen: rich in vitamins and minerals.

Sheep's eyes: a nutrient-rich delicacy (or some people prefer "giant" tuna eyeballs).

Haggis: a traditional Scottish dish where the lining of a sheep's stomach is stuffed with minced sheep's heart, liver, and lungs.

Tripe: the lining of a cow, sheep, or pig's stomach that's usually boiled or stewed.

BON APPÉTIT!

WASTE NOT, WANT NOT

We all try to reduce waste, but did you know how many different parts of an animal can be eaten?

Some people eat chicken feet that have been fried, steamed, or stewed. And despite the hard, thick outer layer of skin, the meat is good for making sauces.

SIDE DISHES

Sheep, cow, and pig's trotters are often boiled to make sauces and stock, and to thicken gravy.

They won't get far walking on those!

FREAKY FACT
Fried pig's ears are crunchy with a chewy middle, while pig's snouts are high in protein and low in fat. Yummy!

ANOTHER COURSE?

"Head cheese" is a dish made from the meats of cow, sheep, and pig's heads, as well as the heart, tongue, and feet. These are all set in gelatin, made by boiling the bones.

You really can eat the whole hog!

"Black pudding" is made by cooking and thickening the blood of a pig, cow, or sheep.

DELICIOUS DELICACIES

These dishes take some preparing . . .

Eat me if you dare!

DID YOU KNOW?
Snake soup is said to be particularly warming in winter. In the US, southern fried rattle snake is said to taste a bit like chicken.

SNAKE-TASTIC

It's not easy to catch and cook a snake, but they remain a popular delicacy in some parts of Asia, such as Vietnam, China, and Malaysia.

While in Indonesia, cobra satay is prepared by soaking snake meat in its blood and bile before roasting on a fire.

DIDDY DUCK

Two-to-three-week-old duck embryos are a unique speciality in some Asian countries, such as Thailand, Laos, and Cambodia.

"Balut" can be boiled and eaten straight from the shell with some seasoning, fried in omelettes, or used as a filling for pastries.

In 2015, the largest serving of balut was recorded when **1,000 pieces** were presented to the town of Pateros in the Philippines.

TASTY TENTACLES

HARD TO SWALLOW! San-nakji is served so fresh that it is sometimes still wriggling on the way down!

If you can stomach a snake, what about a live octopus?

Baby octopus to be exact! San-nakji is a delicacy in Korea. It's said to be mild in flavor but it's best to chew and chew so you don't choke!

DANGER FISH

In Japan, fugu (blowfish or pufferfish) is a dangerous dish—in fact, one wrong move could be deadly!

Parts of the fish, such as the liver, ovaries, and intestines, are highly toxic, and special knives are used to prepare it.

There's no antidote for the poison, but despite the dangers, this expensive dish is very popular —even in the face of death.

No, eat ME if you dare!

TASTY BREW

From craft beers to sports drinks, only the best will do.

TEENY TONICS

In China and Korea, rice wine is often infused with live creatures, such as snakes or two-day-old baby mice, and left to ferment for about a year.

Mouse wine is said to taste like petrol, while snake wine is saltier and fishier.

The wines are drunk as a health tonic, but only once the snake venom has lost its sting.

COFFEE CAT

The world's most expensive coffee, Kopi Luwak, comes from half-digested coffee bean berries that have been eaten and excreted by the Asian palm civet.

This cat-like creature only chooses the ripest berries. As the berries pass through its intestines, they ferment, removing the acidity and making the coffee taste smoother.

You drink what?

WHALE I NEVER

Each year in Iceland, the Thorri festival showcases a unique medieval beer called Hvalur, alongside other ancient delicacies such as fermented shark and cured whale fat.

The beer is said to have a distinct smoky flavor, with a meaty aftertaste . . .

It is made with giant fin whale testicles, each weighing up to 18 lbs, that are smoked with dried sheep dung, then mixed with hops, malted barley, and some of the world's purest water.

DID YOU KNOW?
The story goes that Plantation workers weren't allowed to harvest coffee beans but found these half-digested berries instead and made a tasty brew!

POWER JUICE

The northern giant hornet is feared for its agonizing sting, which has been known to kill.

ACTUAL SIZE!

3 inches

With a wingspan of 3 inches, this creature has remarkable energy and stamina, flying up to 50 miles a day, the equivalent of a human running 2 marathons!

The hornets take food back to their young larvae, who then regurgitate a clear liquid which they feed to their parents.

Hornet Power!

SPORTY HORNETS
This "hornet juice" is full of amino acids, and these have been copied in sports drinks to give us humans a boost, too.

INDEX

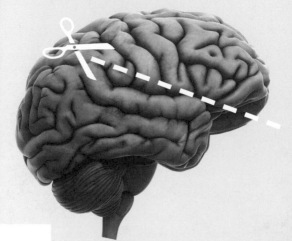

ACKNOWLEDGMENTS

The publishers would like to thank the following sources for their kind permission to reproduce the pictures in this book.
The page numbers for each of the photographs are listed below, giving the page on which they appear in the book and any location indicator (c-center, t-top, b-bottom, l-left, r-right).

7tr, 14t courtesy of the CDC, 47bc courtesy of NASA,

Alamy: 23t Adisha Pramod/Alamy Stock Photo

Creative Commons: 34c FunkMonk, 34bl Hemiauchenia, 36cr, 43br BetacommandBot, 42-43t Handrieu, 51tl, 57 OneThirtySeven, 61t Rama, 65bl MSRau1912

Shutterstock.com: 1 Martina_L, 2 Eric Isselee, 4tr BLACKDAY, 4bl David Calvert, 4bc wearenotebook, 4br wisnupriyono, 5tl Fanfo, 5tc and bc Net Vector, 5tr zcw, 5bl Alexandr Zadiraka, 5bc SciePro, 5br wallybird, 6bl, 8bc Kalcutta, 6br, 11tl Marina Demeshko, 7tl, 13crAnna Shalam, 7bl, 17t khlungcenter, 7br, 18-19 David Calvert, 8bl OHishiapply, 8-9 Juan Gaertner, 9tr NARENTHORN, 9br marigo20, 10 main RichardCH, 10c peipeiro, 10b robuart, 11tr Alex Mit, 11bl Kateryna Kon, 11br Ekaterina Markelova, 12 Olga Bolbot, 13t Roman Samborskyi, 13bl Crevis, 13b alazur, 14bl Macrovector, 15tl Weenee, 15tr PreechaB, 15bl Creativa Images, 15br Christian Schwier, 16t POODPHOTO, 16c somersault1824, 16bl B-D-S Piotr Marcinski, 17bl Brekus, 17cr Hilch, 17br D. Kucharski K. Kucharska, 18b New Africa, 19tr Studio Photo MH, 19b Mario_Hoppmann, 20tl, 22br Aleksandar Dickov, 20bl, 24-25 wearenotebook, 20br, 27 Andrei Nekrassov, 21tl, 28 Cathy Keifer, 21tr, 31br Kuznetsov Alexey, 21bl 31t Videologia, 21br Brian J. Abela, 22t Martina_L, 23cr Frank Fennema, 23bl xpixel, 23br Agussetiawan99, 24-25t Tobias Hauke, 24cl Paulpixs, 25bc Dilen, 25br ijimino, 26t Ethan Daniels, 26br Maria Dryfhout, 27tr Aaronejbull87, 27cl dvlcom - www.dvlcom.co.uk, 29tr Dan Olsen, 29cl kamnuan, 29bl PetlinDmitry, 30t Ali Alawartani, 31tr Danita Delimont, 31c bluedog studio, 32bl S. Aratrak, 32br FotoRequest, 33tl Anna Veselova, 33bl Nick Pecker, 33br Rita_Kochmarjova, 34-35 Brian J. Abela, 35tr CookiesForDevo, 35bl Rvector, 35br Breck P. Kent, 36-37t, 38t pong-photo9, 36bl, 40t Nomad_Soul, 37tr, 46-47t M.Aurelius, 37bl, 45br SciePro, 37br, 49r Vastram, 38c wisnupriyono, 39tr Zern Liew, 39cr Cast Of Thousands, 38cl Trofimov Denis, 39b Kashtal, 40bl Michael Kraus, 40bc Davesayit, 41tr Agussetiawan99, 41cl New Africa, 41br BLACKDAY, 42c Madlen, 42b Pakawat Suwannaket, 43t PixieMe, 44-45 Chatmali, 44bl wonderisland, 45cr Holy Polygon, 46c pics five, 46b bergamont, 47tc oksana2010, 47tr Evikka, 47c NisanatStudio, 47bl Rocksweeper, 48-49 anut21ng Stock, 48c irin-k, 49br Eric Isselee, 50bl, 53t Everett Collection, 50br, 54t Victor1153, 51tr, 61br Alexandr Zadiraka, 51cr, 62-63t Fanfo, 51br, 65tr Alan C. Heison, 52tr Channarong Pherngjanda, 52br andregric and ianakauri, 53c Net Vector, 53b kontur-vid and ksana 777, 54bl Mit Kapevski, 55tr Eric Isselee, 55bl Malgorzata Surawska, 55br Rudmer Zwerver, 56tl CoolKengzz, 56bl cunaplus, 56br Eric Isselee, 57tl Temstock, 57tr PixelSquid3d and Roman Samborskyi, 58tr gillmar and Everett Collection, 58bl gillmar, 59t Bjoern Wylezich, 59cr Everett Collection, 59bl clarst5, 60-61t Everett Collection, 60b Vladimir Gjorgiev, 62b Linda Staf, 63tr Budimir Jevtic, 63bl TTstudio, 63br photomaster, 63cr Eric Isselee, 64t, 64b Andrea Izzotti, 65br Donna Beeler, 66bl, 68-69 Rosa Jay, 66br, 71tl Eric Isselee, 67t, 72-73bl Piyaset, 67tr, 74-75b E-lona, 67bl, 77c SciePro, 67br, 78bl Alexander_Safonov, 68-69 Independent birds, 68cl finchfocus, 69 cr soft_light, 69br Steven Bostock, 70l Aspara liwa and Nadzin, 71bl Gerry Bishop, 71br Natalia Kuzmina, 73tr Art_OLD, 73br Elime, 74t Eileen Kumpf, 75tl Julija Kumpinovica, 75tr Adrian_am13, 75br all_about_people, 76tl cunaplus, 76t photodonato, 76bl, 76br tlgzdmr, 77tl Butus, 77cl Modvector, 77br World_of_Textiles, 78t LightField Studios, 78-79t MR. BUDDEE WIANGNGORN, 79t Alexandra Lande, 79c Loredana Sangiuliano, 79bl s_bukley, 79br Cast Of Thousands, 80tr, 86-87t wallybird, 80bl, 83tr Nick626, 80br, 84 igor.kramar.shots, 81tr, 89tl Zhaskia MD, 81bl, 91br Aries Sutantom 81br, 92-93t PicMy, 82l Moving Moment, 82br Jody Ann, 83cl Vinicius R. Souza, 83cr oksana2010, 83br Fernando Sanchez Cortes, 85tl lucasinapiphotography, 85tr Inna Astakhova, 85cl Sudowoodo, 85br zcw, 86bl LFO62, 87tr Rosa Jay, 87bl Momentum studio, 88l Andrey_Kuzmin, 88-89b Olga_i, 89tr Akarawut, 89c Sergii Koval, 89br Edward Westmacott, 90l kwanchai.c, 90c Eric Isselee, 91tr overkit, 91cl RDRBrust, 91cr cherry-hai, 91bl krit_manavid, 92bl peampath2812, 92-93b dwi putra stock, 93tr akiyoko, 93cr kirpmun, 93bl Thaninee Chuensomchit, 93br Asier Romero, 94tc Aries Sutanto, 94bl SciePro, 94br Vladimir Gjorgiev, 95t Roman Samborskyi, Craig Rus-sell, 96 Videologia

Every effort has been made to acknowledge correctly and contact the source and/or copyright holder of each picture. Any unintentional errors or omissions will be corrected in future editions of this book.